❖ENCORE❖

A COLLECTION OF POEMS

RUSS PEERY

authorHOUSE®

AuthorHouse™
1663 Liberty Drive
Bloomington, IN 47403
www.authorhouse.com
Phone: 1 (800) 839-8640

Published by AuthorHouse 08/10/2016

ISBN: 978-1-5246-1807-0 (sc)
ISBN: 978-1-5246-1806-3 (e)

Library of Congress Control Number: 2016911208

Print information available on the last page.

This book is printed on acid-free paper.

ENCORE

CONTENTS

FOREWORD

Four years ago I wrote a Foreword to my "last book of poems." Not long thereafter my eager editor began to set up the beginnings of this collection, called ENCORE. This book has only become a reality because of the energy of Joanne Schwandes. I have less of that than before, but can't stop writing—just because I can't. The process always seems a bit presumptuous— that I assume there are folks out there interested in what's in my head which I then translate onto paper. But that is how it feels to me.

Twenty years ago I became serious about writing poetry—and only because my mother urged me on just before she died. I had written a few things before that time, but only then did I feel some necessity to get more involved with musing. And I have been blessed beyond measure for I've been able to stay at it for all this time.

Russ Peery
21 June 2016
Kissimmee FL

WALKERS OF THE DAWN

A DOSE OF DAWN

The sunlight
which strikes my eyes at dawn
bears its surprises.

Never the same
when it returns again—
on that I can depend.

Of course some days are dark
even when the night departs
and ushers in a dreary day.

I walk into the early mornings
amazed, sometimes
that I'm still here to gaze
upon this sky and earth.

It's worth so much for me
to see our days begin
and though there are those
who do not welcome them
I recommend a dose of dawn.

Swallowed by a waiting heart
it might part a sea of darkness
and enable one to smile—
at least a little while.

A GIFT FROM THE RISING SUN

In the east
in the early morning
it seemed as if the sun
was striving to break through
the hovering gray clouds
and could not part them—
could only make the sky
a little brighter.

A spot of gold appeared—
but very dim and fading—
then reappearing.

It seemed suggesting
that sometimes it's hard to rise—
that the sun can emulate
some folks I know
who do not easily
rise and shine.

They bide their time
then slowly join the human race.

That's how
the sun appeared to me that day—
its gift to me a metaphor
for folks I love.

DIFFERENT KINDS OF SILENCE

How your house feels
after the grandchildren have gone home.

How you wonder what they are doing
when your grandchildren are in a room
for ten minutes and are quiet.

How you feel when, in a crowded restaurant
you remove your hearing aids.

How, when walking in the rain
the sound made on your umbrella
removes all other sounds.

How the angels sing quietly
when at dawn
you open your door to the east
and see a crescent moon rising.

You may have your own named silences—
at least that's what I assume and hope for.

DAWN'S PUDDLES

Walking
toward mud puddles at dawn—
then viewing them sideways
after a storm has cleared
is something some folks do—
but likely, just a few.

At first the puddles appear black—
they then turn gray
and start reflecting telephone poles
(some of them, their lights turn off
as the dawn turns brighter).

They then display
tree tops and roof tops.
And last, the sky
with floating clouds.

Quite suddenly, it's over
and all that's left are puddles
that settle on the road
looking not interesting at all—
and as something to avoid
if one's not young and playful.

WALKERS OF THE DAWN

We walkers of the dawn
must readjust our walking times
to coincide with earth's demands.

This time of year we start our journeys
a little later every morning.

We feel the cosmic shrinking light
and wallow in our knowledge
while sleepers go on sleeping
waiting for their digitals
to tell them when to rise.

MIST GHOSTS

When I walked by the lake
early one morning
mist ghosts were hovering
and walking on the water
just like Jesus did—
long time ago.

Back then he wasn't called
The Holy Ghost.
That came later
when church folk
invented names
to deal with the ineffable.
I see what I can't understand
most every day—
the world's alive with mystery.

ONE ORDINARY MORNING

The dawn mist
hovered over the ground
hiding tree trunks
but not their upper branches.

Above the trees
blue skies were emerging.

And then the setting moon appeared—
was just about to disappear.

I turned around and faced the east
and found a sunrise spatter painting
with its golden brush.

I could hardly hold my ecstasy.
All of it seemed too much
for my meager mortal heart.

I was glad there were no mountains—
glad there were no flowing streams
or water falls.

A man can only handle
so much beauty
in an ordinary morning.

RUNNING

The other day
my nose ran
as I was walking.

My nose doesn't walk
and I don't run anymore
much to my distress.

I need a handkerchief
more than I need track shoes.

But as we are prone to say
these days:
"It goes with the territory."

I walk now with some ease
and scuffle only occasionally.

How long good mobility
will accompany my longevity
is a matter that sometimes
runs through my mind
as I take my walks in the morning.

SO FLED THE NIGHT

As dawn began to light the eastern sky
it seemed that it was only I was walking by
the shadowed places that I know so well—
the places I have chosen there to dwell.

And when the quarter moon I didn't know
was in the east, suddenly began to glow
as it slipped out from beneath a cloud
it startled me. My mind had not allowed

for moonlight to be a portion of my day
yet how I welcomed it and made my way
with unexpected joy. And then the east
took on a radiance. This celestial feast

was almost more than I could take. My sight
was overwhelmed at dawn. So fled the night.

THE HONEYMOON OF POSSIBILITIES

It occurred to me
when I saw
the beautiful morning sky
just before the sunrise
turn so bland
just after the sun did rise
that many of our dreams
are better before fulfillment
and many of our hopes
become tarnished
after they are realized.
Let me call this:
"The Honeymoon of Possibilities."

Even so
there are dreams and hopes
that exceed their purveyor's plans.
The sky can do this, too
and it does this sometimes
when I'm taking a morning walk.

THE INCIPIENT SKY

I opened our front door
at quarter of six in the morning.

Stepping across the threshold
I bent down and picked up
THE ORLANDO SENTINEL.

I then looked up and saw
a quarter moon
on top of the pre-dawn sky
doing its best to stay bright
amidst some fading stars.

I chose to keep looking up
even as my fingers tore the plastic
surrounding the news of the day.

The news could wait, I thought
but the moon could not.

So I set the paper down
and walked into the early light—
dim and beautiful
and bidding farewell to the night.

So soon in that incipient day
could I begin to count my blessings.

THE NEW DAY

The new day, I hope
will make itself ready for me—
its light just right—
not too bright.
A few stars left—
and even the moon, sometimes—
the sun still a distance from rising.
The birds will be at it—
chattering or singing
covering
some distant traffic sounds.
It is best that it be
a little cool
calling for a light jacket.
Yes, I could be in another place
where violence is near—
where there are no pleasant paths.
And I know some folks
unable to venture into the dawn.
But right now
it is only I—
the one who will open my door
and I will find pleasure
out there beyond it
where I will try to measure
every good thing.

THE SILVER SLIVER

The silver sliver of the crescent moon
sought out my eyes
just as the sky released its darkness
and allowed the blue invasion.

It tipped slightly to the south
appearing as if
it were pouring beauty
into the east
where cloud smudges of pink
awaited its arrival.

I saw another walker
and said "Look!"

He turned around
and found what
he had nearly missed.

Sometimes all it takes
is turning
when someone's near
to show us
what we might have been denied.

THE VOICE OF THE DAWN

Sometimes the dawn comes
whispering.

I am always listening
and I am intrigued by its voice
speaking to my eyes.

Sometimes its brilliant colors in the east
seem to shout so much beauty
I can hardly take it in.

The sounds strangely come to me
while I am looking.

In those moments
when I am out waiting for
the beginning of a new day
sight tends to make sounds.

WHEN MORNING BREAKS

Morning breaks into the eastern sky
and I, old man, have not ceased to wonder why
I still find fascination in the sunrise.

The world's agenda seldom mars the pleasure
offered each day, though I cannot measure
one against the other—they're all treasures.

At times I've missed the rendezvous with dawn.
Though mostly it's together we belong
there are intrusions; and when, it feels quite wrong.

The daily news that lies upon our sidewalk
I ignore, as well as television's talk.
Later I'll absorb them—but first I balk.

Heaven first, as I begin my mornings
then I'll deal with all the daily warnings.
May they find me ready and not wanting.

AT LEAST A LITTLE WHILE

I saw Wordsworth's "lonely cloud"
wandering in the eastern sky
waiting for the sun to rise.

It took on portions of its glorious light
while I, in shadows strewn by night
began to feel them disappear around me.

That cloud became a harbinger
that guaranteed another day for me.

To my delight I watched the transformation—
my fascination guaranteed to last
at least a little while.

CELESTIAL DELIGHTS

A CASUALTY OF LUNAR LOVE

When the digital clock
by the side of the bed
"struck" 6:00, I rose
to sit on the edge of the bed—
and rose some more
and opened the blinds.

There was the full moon
setting.

I expected it to be there
and it was—
just a round, bright disc
about to fall
into the tops of trees.

I always feel
that the moon is interested in me.

I am a casualty of lunar love
and though I know
there is no reciprocity
I'm always prone to think there is
when I am alone with the moon.

A PACT WITH CLOUDS

We may lack mountains here
but we have clouds
that sometimes make them.

In fact, the clouds make many things
of which we are deprived.

But one must
make a pact with clouds
with one's imagination
and then "the sky's the limit."

Not every day, of course
can we request a sight
and have it come before the night.

But if we look upon our canopy
with open minds and hearts
soon we will see unfold our fantasy.

The clouds and I conspire
to build a world that I desire
when I am bound by circumstance
to travel less than I did once.

HAIKU

Most days I like to look up at the clouds
my back upon the earth and my eyes upon the sky.
Peace comes to me horizontally.

I pass the house, empty now of friends
and feel within an emptiness exceeding expectations.
I think that I'll not pass that way again.

The quiet surface of a nearby lake
showed me the sky. I tiptoed slowly to the water's edge
and saw an old man framed in blue, with clouds.

CELESTIAL DELIGHTS

The moon sliver
stole the eastern sky
as its darkness turned to gray—
the beginning of my day
before agenda claimed my hours.

How fortunate I am to see
the frequent offerings of the sky
denied to folks
who can't get up
or won't get up
to view the turning of the world
with its celestial delights
when dawn appears.

ONE DAY

THE EARLY MORNING SKY

   WAS LIKE MY

FOUR-YEAR-OLD GRANDSON

HAD PAINTED IT

WITH FELT MARKERS.

CLOUD THERAPY

I lay upon my chaise—
and swung my legs around
off the ground—
got close to being horizontal.

I set my outdoor thermostat
to seventy-nine. That's fine.
Wind speed between five and seven—
that's about its speed in heaven.

Then, with blue sky overhead
I started hanging white, puffy clouds—
not just one lonely one—that's no fun.
How about three or four or even more?

I looked around and then closed my eyes
and rhymes begin dancing in my head—
and more than two or three:
sky-high
heaven-seven
spaghetti-confetti
lobster-mobster.

I did not stop at those—more arose.
So I opened my eyes
and to my surprise
there were no more rhymes.

And I had a great time
just watching clouds.

DID YOU EVER?

Did you ever see
the clouds swallow a setting sun?

Well I did, just west of here
where I often watch
some great displays of color.

I've seen all kinds of settings
and I'm betting that what I saw
is most unusual.

Dark purple clouds
playing on the horizon
suddenly made a mouth
just south of a group of palms
and gulped down
that hot star with ease.

It pleased me so
I've recorded it for history.

I WANT THE SKY TO BE

I want the sky to be
the way it was to me
when I was very young—
a canopy of blue
that let the stars through
when it turned dark.

And the sun came up
and the sun went down.

And the moon came up
and the moon went down
but changed its shape.

That was my astronomy
when I was two or three
or maybe more—
perhaps four.

It has changed since then
and by the time I was ten
all of that disappeared.

Maybe
when I'm very old
the sky will be
like it used to be
when I was three.
I'll wait and see
if it comes back to me.

IT IS POSSIBLE

It is possible that
one of my grandfathers
or one of my great-grandfathers
who were all likely alive in 1912
were as intrigued by the crescent moon
that graced the dawn of the mid-April sky—
were moved to know the same ecstasy
as I often know
when I see a new day born in this particular way.

It is possible that
one of them later learned
that there were lifeboats filled
with desperate folks who saw the same moon
just after they watched the Titanic
vanish into the sea—
moonlight and starlight reflected
into their fearful eyes.

It is possible that
at least one of them
was amazed
as I am
how the best and worst of life
flourishes
beneath the same sky
at the same time.

JUST ANOTHER DAY

A narrow strip—
a narrow stripe
of orange
stretched along
the east
and that is what I saw
as I began my walk
the other day.

It grew in length and breadth
with every step I took
and soon it lost its stripness
or its stripeness
and became a mass of orange
that stole the show that morning.

Yes, just another day
began for me—
just another day.

LONG STREAKS OF GOLD

It was disappointing.

The sunset show
received a blow
as a curtain of dark clouds
began dispelling possibilities
for our seeing
another beautiful descent.

But
just before we left the scene
long streaks of gold
began to appear in the west
slicing the gray into pieces.

We were surprised
and did not turn away.

We stayed a little longer
lingering
before twilight came
happy that our expectations
had been fulfilled.

SUNRISE AS HONEYMOON

When "first light"
began to reach the eastern clouds
there was an explosion of pink
that spread before my eyes
that took my breath away.

As the clouds began to scatter
they turned to silver for a little while
and then they took on the color gold
that seemed even more impressive
than the many streaks of silver.

When the rising sun became a fireball
much of the enchantment disappeared
and likely, the best that it could do
was continue warming earth
and surely that is not a simple feat.

"The best" of watching East is often first
so I enjoy it while it lasts.

The solar honeymoon is frequent
for it returns and then returns
and then returns again.

We have so many second chances
offered by our amazing sky.

THE CLOUDS AS ACTORS

As dawn creeps into day
the eastern clouds pretend
that they're a mountain range
just above the tops of trees.

Then they pretend
that they've been finger-painted
by little ones who think
the sky's an easel:
blue and red—orange and green.
My what a scene!

And then they fall apart
and start to climb the canopy
beneath which they employ
their magic right before my eyes.

And then they're white
and take the shapes of animals
which parade across the sky.

Their stage is easily accessed.
Their shows are different every day
and no one has to pay.

THE CLOUDS DRESS SUNLIGHT

Just think how it would be
if the sun's rays
did not ever wear clouds.

Sometimes they come to us
absolutely naked
and that is about as appealing
as I would be
were I to walk down the street
with nothing on.

The clouds make a great wardrobe
for the sun's journey—
especially when it appears
after a long night
or when it leaves us
at the end of an ordinary day.

Of course
sometimes they're too much
and overwhelm the light.

But mostly we appreciate
how the clouds dress sunlight.

THE MOON'S HIDING PLACES

The moon told me "I have four places I hide."—
and he told me with his crescent smile.
I think you know how it beguiles.

"I hide in the shadow of the earth—
sometimes just parts of me are glowing—
and sometimes none of me is showing."

"I hide in the blue when the sun is out.
Unless you study the sky carefully
there's not a bit of me you'll see."

"I hide when I slide beneath the horizon.
Folks say they see the moon go down
but it's really the earth that's spinning around."

"I hide above thick clouds sometimes
and though you'd like to see me shine
that decision isn't even mine."

The moon has much to say to me.
He helps me be. He helps me be.

WHERE I SEE CHOREOGRAPHED

Near nine p.m.
on the first day of July
light from the setting quarter moon
mingled with the western twilight.

I delighted in this ambience
to the point of being overwhelmed—
all this from my window
where I see choreographed
on so many nights
celestial wonders
that adorn my simple world.

EMOTIONS

AN AWFUL THOUGHT

If deprived of keyboard
pencils, pen and ink
what would I think?
What would I do?
I'd likely stew and stew.
The threat
is only in my mind
but if its kind were real
I don't know how I'd deal.

As much as I am
bound to the dear woman
who's bound to me
am I tied to what
my fingers offer me—
tools that extract
the essence of
my meandering mind
and allow its sharing.

God forbid my losing
what has come to be
the means by which
I nurture who I am.

BROODING

Most of us are not immune to brooding—
when one feels that there's no hope intruding
and the sky looks dark despite the sun.
Whatever blessed one seems forever done.

Though one might try to move his thoughts away
from sadness, he's helpless to control his day
and it unfolds as if he were a hostage
to the bleakness he can hardly manage.

When the brooding wilts, or how it does
is often mysterious. One wonders why it was
and isn't any more. Perhaps a prayer—
perhaps attention by a friend who cared.

Are there those who never entertain
the gloom—who think of sunshine—never rain?

COURTING NOSTALGIA

There are moments when I savor memories.

I pull them from a reservoir so deep—
one that's deepened over many years.

I have a habit: returning to the was
because what is is sometimes not enough
to satisfy my longings—nor does it require
the aptitudes I used to have and need
and which I now can set aside most days
and court nostalgia as if it were a bride
waiting for my wistful overtures.

CONSCIOUSLY CONNIVE

The way I see it now
is not the way I saw it then.

Back then I wanted to be noticed.

All through my time in school
I wanted to be noticed—
to have a piece of popularity.

I wasn't an athlete.
I am better looking now than then—
never got elected to anything—
didn't even get THE BEST HAIR
in our 1945 year book.

I assumed that that was how it was
and always would be throughout my life—
that I'd be deprived of accolades.

When I chose to be a preacher
I did not consciously connive
to change these matters.
I was into theology
and I assumed that I'd find God.

But I found other things
and maybe God found me.

Preachers too easily become
the center of attention
for so many folks.

I was surprised
when things began to change for me.

It got so I had to learn
not to inhale the accolades.

And I am not sure
I ever learned completely.

FEELING OBSOLETE

I'm not sure
when it first started—
feeling obsolete.
Fairly recently, I believe.
The feeling comes and goes
triggered, in part
by the morning's SENTINEL
and the evening's TV news
and by views shown me
by my bathroom's mirror.
There are others nearby
who must sometimes
feel the same as I.
Likely, those feelings
will come to me
until the day I die—
that day when I'll discover
if there's more in store for me.

GET OVER IT!!!

When you have walked the corridors of time
for years and years, and admit to modest fears
of the unknown, you will likely find
another—a friend who will offer you his ear

as you give voice to your contemplations
usually withheld. You do not face with ease
the possibilities of your continuation
when you see so much that does not please.

Some folks have had so much with which to cope
leaving you to shudder at their dealings.
Such unfolding tends to shatter hope
for ease at endings—an unpleasant feeling.

Banish thoughts which tend to harvest gloom.
Your end may come tomorrow. Is that too soon?

HANDLING MANY YEARS

How am I going to handle old age?

I'll let you know in a little while.

I'd like to stay around
and be able to tell you, but...

Anyway, I'm still working on it.

I seem to get a hold of it
and then it changes—
often to my surprise.

It's not only heavy, it's slippery.

And I note that
the challenges some folks face
appear to be handled easily
yet others with the same agenda
seem overwhelmed.

Go figure!

Some days I feel lucky.

Some days I just feel old.

HOW DO I FEEL?

How do I feel
when my friends are shoveling snow
and here there is grass to grow?
And whether it grows fast or slow
it isn't I who mows.

How do I feel
when many a friend is ill
and I am sort of healthy still
though I've signed my living will
and occasionally take a pill?

How do I feel
when the world is such a mess—
at least that's what the news suggests
and I do nothing I must confess
and I scarcely ever stress?

I surely feel quite fortunate
and I know I don't deserve it.
I can't figure it out one little bit
that I've not been harder hit.
The blessings do not seem to fit.

I GET OVER IT

I'd like to have
more energy.

It's plain to see
that that's unlikely.

And I confess:
my prowess
is less
than what it was—
and this distresses me.

Oh, I can rage
about old age.

Can you assuage me?

I'm no sage, for sure.

Indeed
I ain't no saint—
but I've complaints
about what years can do.

Do you?

Do you ever stew
as I do?

Know that I'll get over it
by writing just a bit.

I NO LONGER SEEK TO PLEASE

Does someone read my lines
and fail to understand?

I know that I read lines
and find my comprehension taxed
while others read those lines
applauding as they do.

And they might scan my poems
and take a dim view of my muse.

It's hard for me to tell
just where I fit
within the panoply of words
that line so many pages.

I think that once I sought some praise
for my delineations
but I no longer seek to please one
other than myself.

I STRIVE FOR EMPATHY

Early in the morning
I encounter spider webs—
on the bridge I walk upon—
beneath some live oak trees
as well.

They stick upon my forehead—
my arms and legs.
Not many, to be sure
but just enough to let me know
that some creatures
were there first
amidst the places that I walk.

The webs, they stick to me—
and they annoy me.

When I quickly brush them off
I feel some more.

They're not lethal, to be sure
and I never see them
nor the spinners of the night
but I feel their touch
before I rub them off.

How I effect their mornings
destroying their labors
I do not know
nor do I know their size or shape
or their longevity.

I strive for empathy
knowing that I likely bother them
more than they bother me.

I WATCH TV

I'm amazed
that I can see
so many tragedies
and then get on with life
without a thought of
what my eyes and ears
absorbed so recently.

I watch TV
and that is how
it works for me.

And I suspect
that you're the same as I—
that you can get exposed
to so much pain
and even if you wince
that you'll return again
to what you were
before a channel
offered you catastrophes.

If we didn't have immunity
from exposures to the vast array
of human suffering
we'd likely weep and weep
and drown ourselves in tears.

INSPIRATION

Some wait for inspiration
while others plunge ahead
knowing not what they'll create
but feel that they have a date—
a deadline that they need to meet.

I'm one of those
who does not wait
but bring an empty page
before my eyes
and try to build a poem
with whatever's in my head.

It may be a poor way to proceed
but if I postponed the writing
until something exciting
came to grasp my simple mind
I might be lingering forever
and the fingering of my computer
I most likely would decline.

So I approach the Muse with pleading
before proceeding
and occasionally the Muse responds.

But even if we seldom meet
the exercise can still be sweet
and does but little harm.

NIGHTLY MARINADE

Every night
I try to marinate my mind
with many a delicious thought:
gratitude for many things
and hopefulness
for things to come.

Sometimes
I am quite successful—
at other times
I feel I've failed
to add the proper spices.

How much this marinade
impacts my sleep
I do not really know.

I like to think
it matters much
and that it even helps
the dreaming that I do
before the night is done.

You might call this prayer
or efforts of the mind
to help one cope with dailyness.

I don't really care about its name
but I hope that
you might do the same.

PLAYING WITH "SELF-PITY"

Visited by a modicum of self-pity
while laid way back in my recliner
I say to me: "I am useless!"

And then I raise the question with myself:
"Does that mean I am worthless?"

I decide that there is a difference
between being useless and worthless.

That distinction was new to me—
meaning I never considered it
until that very moment.

I can still be worth something
and yet be useless.

That means to me that
"Somebody must love me"
and I have no doubt but that
somebody does.

They love me
even if self-pity
plays around with my inner self.

QUIET

Quiet can sometimes be
one of the gifts of deafness.

It is often sought
by those whose noisy worlds
bombard them to distraction.

But quiet can also make for loneliness
for those impaired by slowly losing
their sensitivity to sound.

Silence can sometimes sour
for one deprived
of verbal human touching.

SADNESS COMES

Sometimes the sadness comes
and you wonder where it came from.
There may seem to be no particular sorrow
other than you know
that there is always some, somewhere.

Sometimes the sadness comes
and you are well aware
of news too close to you
not to be consumed when sorrow
grasps your heart.

The years don't seem to offer wisdom
of how to deal with either one—
that's just the way it is—
the way it will be
a little while longer.

SEARCHING FOR A RAINBOW

I ran into the yard
for it was raining hard
and yet the sun was out.

I had hoped
to see a rainbow
for I know
that sunshine and the rain
so often build one.

I searched the sky
and don't know why
it wasn't anywhere.

It's not the only thing
I hoped might be
that left me disappointed.

SIXTY SECONDS EXPANDING

Waiting for
the one you love
to come home—
to come home
to the home
you have made
over so many years—
this is not unusual.

But when that loved one
does not arrive on time—
when the expected rendezvous
does not occur
worry begins to intrude—
slowly, at first—
and then the minutes grow longer.

Strange how that can be—
sixty seconds expanding.

But they do
and I know that this is true.

SLAINED ARROGANCE

He was not
prone toward bragging
but he made one exception:
"I've used woodworking
power tools
for nearly fifty years
and still have all my fingers!"

Whatever arrogance he had
was slain by a table saw
that hungered for his thumb
and damn near got it.

And there was lots of blood!

THAT'S THE WAY IT IS

"That's the way it is"
I hear a lot these days
as folks attempt
to sum it up, then let it go
as if we have
the satisfactory explanation
and have no need
for further comment.

It probably has to do
with resignation and
dismissing possibilities
for change.

I have embraced the thought
when I've felt close
to being overwhelmed
but when I've backed away from that
I feel as if I still have freedom
to change a thing or two.

THE FEAR OF LETTING GO

When
I saw the moon
hanging on a cloud
as it set in the west
it looked like
it didn't want to
drop into the horizon.

I think it hung on
for fear of letting go.
And if it hesitated
I understand.

THE LAST IN LINE

Somebody always has to be
the last in line.

It is recess time in the spring.
Two self-appointed captains
with athletic prowess
begin their choosing.

Of course, they want the best
and then the near best
and on and on 'til there's no one left—
or hardly anyone left
to fall in line behind those chosen.

In my particular class
I was not fast
and thus was often chosen last.

Being one of those
familiar with that kind of "last"
I know that memory haunts
for decades.

And now I'm nearly last in line
of those chosen by the Grim Reaper.
There may be some levity
in my longevity.

THE MANTLE OF SELF-PITY

The mantle of self-pity
hangs nearby
and I am tempted
to put it on
and whine a bit—
but then I refrain.

Desiring to rid myself of it
I take it to the Thrift Store
and I offer the mantle
to the folks who tend
to sorting and to selling.

They tell me
they have too many
and can use no more.

So I still have it
too nearby and too easy
for me to reach.

I pray for strength
to resist its warmth
and time will tell
if I'm strong enough to cope
without that mantle.

VENGEANCE

There are some feelings
that you might have sometime
that you are not proud of—
and you may not be able
to abolish them
even if you wish you could.

I was a weak little boy
and could not much compete
with my peers—
not exceedingly incapable—
but just enough so
that I was very aware
of my limitations.

But, I am a fairly strong old man
and if I could
I would return to my childhood days
and I would show my little friends
that my life didn't end
because I couldn't compete back then.

If any of them are still around
they might hear the sound of my crowing
knowing that if I could
I would take them on.

THE VASTNESS OF AN ORDINARY MAN

Down in the recesses of my mind
where so many memories dwell
I call on them sometimes
to entertain my waning self.

Sometimes the most beautiful
are sad
and I cannot dwell on them too long
lest I wallow in despair.

However, to avoid them altogether
is to deny my past.

But the sad ones do not last
for the joyful ones intrude
and set a different mood in me
and I can almost recapture ecstasy.

And when the show is over
and there are duties to be done
I find a moment here and there
to be amazed at what's been harvested
and remains so plentiful—
the vastness of an ordinary man.

WE MOURN A LITTLE LIZARD

"His eye is on the sparrow"
scripture suggests
and I suggest
"His eye is not on the lizard."
A little lizard crept into
the circuitry of our AC
and there he died
not privy to the information
that he was in a place of danger.

We did not know
that lizards often are disruptive
to the coolness man desires
but now we know
and mourn a little lizard.

THE ZOOEY ZOO

It was a zoo!
That is the zoo
some sixty miles away:
babies galore
and kids of every age
and shape and size
and scattered
moms and dads
and some animals, too.

They (except for the animals)
swarmed all over
and I was there
in the midst of the swarm
feeling old—feeling
"Oh, sooo old!"
and though
the many there
paid me no heed
I paid them plenty
and you can believe
I felt most relieved
when I escaped
and returned to the place
where the old folks live.

THE TREES IN THE WEST

It was as if the trees in the west were hungry
and their windblown leaves were tongues
that reached up into the sky, salivating.

They licked the sun rays then began to devour
them.

Slowly they were swallowing the sun
and I watched it disappear
into the stomach of the night.

But before the total darkness came the twilight
and again my delight at the turning of the earth.

FOLKS I KNOW

A LEGACY

I trust Hana found the rattle tasted good—
was told she also shook it—
listened to the sound it made.
She wrote to me the other day
with some help from her mother
telling me that she was glad I'd made it
for her little hands to grasp—
for her little mouth to taste.
And I was pleased that what I'd made
provided her some happiness.

I started making rattles in the eighties
and have not ceased to craft them
though my production rate has slowed
as I've grown old. If I have no other legacy than this:
that I have made ten thousand babies smile
then my life has been worthwhile.

AMEN!

So much will happen in the world today.
So much agenda for the one who prays.
I'll get on my knees but do not plan to stay.

I'll try this: "Lift up your eyes unto the hills."
Possibly I'll transcend my doctor bills
and think only of my body's ills.

Or better yet, I'll try to think of others.
Though gone, I often think about my mother.
I have a sister still, but never had a brother.

Then there are those to whom I'm not related
who, by chance or guidance have congregated
with me—our lives for good or ill fated.

I'll speak to heaven of my concern for them
as I do daily—on that you can depend.
And then I think my prayers will finally end.
Perhaps I'll add: "AMEN!"

COMPARISONS

There are folks I know
who are better off than I:
fiscally and physically.

There are folks I know
who are worse off than I
fiscally and physically.

I am in the middle
it seems to me.

Comparisons get more tricky
when you think:
socially—
mentally—
spiritually.

I do not claim that I excel
in these categories
nor would I see myself
deficient.

But my mind sometimes
enters these arenas
and I play with them.

Comparisons sometimes
are odious
and I best leave them be
to others—not to me.

EDITOR AS PREDATOR

My editor
is like a predator
circling my work
checking
the already-checked spelling
and searching for
the proper margins
and the proper spacing
and the proper size of letters
that may someday be a book.
She creates slots
for my various themes.
She's kind of a machine
that fastens onto every word
and likes my words to be heard
so she reads them to her mother.
Could there be another
who would pay such strict attention
to my overtures made verbal?
I am grateful
for this editor
and I credit her
for expanding my horizons.

I HOPE THAT SHE WILL FIND A POET

I was allowed to read her poem
written for Mother's Day.

She rhymed mothers with brothers and smothers-
lunch with munch.

Unwritten
but totally there
was love.

I who had never met her nor her mother
until that night just a few days ago
just loved that poem.

The poet is eleven
and I hope that there will be more from her—
her journey still young.
What will she be like when she is my age—
and her world?

I hope that she will find a poet
the age she is now.

She now calls me
MR. RUSS.

IT TOOK A WHILE

We began to talk
about our early days—
days now long ago
and far away.
My sister still lived
where we had gone to school—
one brick building—
twelve years.
She knew about the living and the dying
in our home town.
I was amazed—
there were so many
who no longer were!
When I lay down to go to sleep
I had to process all those losses
I had heard about from her.
It took a while.
It took a while.

MY SISTER AND I

She paints.
She paints with paints.
She's my sister.
She's older than I.
Now, that's really old!

I paint, too.
But I paint with words.
I don't need brushes.
I need only the keyboard
on this laptop.
No messy brushes
and I can easily delete.
And I do, often, and
rewrite, trying again.
'til I am satisfied.

My sister is
interested in light
and shape and color.
She's gone at it
quite a while now
and actually makes money
from her paintings.

I don't, from my poems.
I suppose I could envy that
but I'm proud of her
and don't feel myself
to be in competition.

My interest is in
translating what I see and
feel
into the kind of writing
that lets a reader know
what I perceive.

We both have found
much pleasure
in our parallel pursuits
and we will persist
as long as time permits.

PINK

I'm 87 and
have never had
my fingernails painted.

When she asked me:
"What color?"
I said "Pink."

She turned 4 this summer
and became a beautician
on Christmas day.

The polish will fade away
but will stay long enough
for me to savor a memory.

RAY DOWD

My memories do not encompass
heroes, or good friends
or noble deeds
when I consider
what this day means.

For much of my life
on this day of remembrance
I've returned to Ray Dowd—
a kid two years older than I
who was the first to die
from my home town
in the Greatest War.

I did not know him well.

He never had a chance
to do so many of the things
I've taken for granted—
choosing, choosing, choosing.

It's coming to an end—
my quotidian dailyness.

In some miniscule way
I know that Ray Dowd
has helped to shape my life.

SUDDENLY

I did the usual morning things:
a little walking and rowing—
some coffee with the one
who loves me best of all.

Nothing particular awaited our day—
just its usual hours unfolding.

I open our email—
and suddenly, as I read it
my mind travels to
where a friend of ours has fallen—
a seriously fractured hip.

Beyond our concern
I recall being told
that when the elderly fall
they are often writing
the last chapter of their lives.

No longer were we pondering
our quotidian plans for the day.

We talked about our friend.
and we discussed our own fears
which cause us to be extra careful.

When I step into the bathtub
at day's end
I hang on tightly to the bars
installed there
to keep my aging safe.

THE MAGNETIC POEM

I don't know when
refrigerators and magnets
first started their love affairs
but well before
this century's beginnings
they clung to one another
savoring not their strong ties
but offering a willingness
to uphold the things
that people savor:
photos, clippings from newspapers,
shopping lists, and even poems.

When a woman told me
that she posted one of my poems
on her refrigerator
I felt truly complimented.

Whether or not it's still there I'm unaware.
And I'll never be able to find out
for I've forgotten who she is.

THE SCISSORS CUTTING GRASS

She was not a little girl
nor was she a big one—
but somewhere in-between
when, one day she came home
after having been away at camp.

As she walked the walk
familiar because of so much repetition
she noticed there was something wrong—
the grass had grown so long—
the grass had grown so long
much longer than her neighbor's lawn.

So she got herself some scissors
and began to cut that lengthy grass.
That seemed to be
the best that she could do.

And so she cut and cut and cut
until her mother came from work
and saw her only daughter
on her knees and clipping—
on her knees and snipping.

This story has an end
but its ending has been lost.
for memory discards so much
that it regards as trivial,

But the scissors cutting grass—
they'll be there, almost forever.

THE SLUG

There was a slug who
lived beneath a log.

There was a woman, a teacher
who was quite enamored with
the creatures we call slugs.

She taught nature to
a group of three year olds.

One day that teacher
followed by her class of little ones
"just happened" to roll away
a nearby log
beneath which
the slug that I have mentioned
lived.

There was great excitement all around—
the teacher and the children—
although the slug remained indifferent.

The little ones came close to it
and were allowed to handle it.

They learned more about a slug
(though they were only three)
than I ever gleaned in all my many years.

And if they ever came
to learn from me
they'd gain some knowledge
of a sluggish man.

THE YOUNG DRIVER

When she first
squirreled her way
into our Versa
it was the steering wheel
she grabbed.

But soon she became intrigued
with various levers:
the windshield wipers
and the signal lights.

Then it was the horn—it made her smile—
then the radio and AC.

She was disallowed access to the starter
but that didn't seem to matter.

The windows going up and down
brought further smiles.

She claims this car when it becomes her visitor—
every couple of weeks.

She puts on her grandfather's sun glasses—
her final overture.

It lasts a little while
and takes no gas
to bring such satisfaction.

TOUCHING

Keep in touch.
That was touching.
He has the touch.
Some people touch too much—
some hardly ever do.

Our doctor's touching
is absolutely just right.

He knows how to do it
so that you know he cares.

And though in a given day
he may have touched many
before he moves toward you
the move he makes
is just for you and no other.

You move from
being an object of his concern
to being a subject, in an instant.

You talk to others about him
and they feel the same.

You need not know his name
but know we're glad
we came to see him
some years ago
for we have been deeply touched—
again and again.

HARVESTING A MEMORY

A MEMORY REVIVED

The shadow of a cloud
moved across the grass.

I watched it pass.

And after it passed
it became a pleasant memory—
and then it became a forgotten memory
for my mind let go of it
to tend to other matters
requiring my employment.

But now that cloud shadow
has become a memory revived
for it has been re-captured with my pen
and I've allowed you entree
into one of the shadows of my mind
that does not resemble darkness.

A PANOPLY OF PHOTOGRAPHS

So many of them
posted on our refrigerator—
snapshots, some with curled edges
hung up there with various little magnets
which keep portions of our history
from falling to the kitchen floor—
reminders of the past—
many of friends who long ago or recently
left our troubled world too soon.
Those pictures aren't consulted every day
but are pointed to
when certain friends come by
and show an interest in this display.
We are most pleased to share
these connections to our past.
And some of those who look today
may become looked at tomorrow—
will join our panoply of photographs
attached to doors we open every day.

A PARTICULAR PLEASURE

There was a time
not very long ago
when I took pleasure
in imagining folks
opening up some gifts
and finding work that I had made
and sent off to some craft shops.

Especially at Christmas
when I knew
the things that I had made
were scattered
all around our country
and were likely gift wrapped—
perhaps with bows adorning them.

Now that particular pleasure
is mostly gone
but I'm still able to pull it up
from my assorted memories
and smile a little.

A VETERAN NEVER TESTED

I can generate laughter
when I tell about my sea duty
as Seaman First Class:
driving a truck from Brooklyn—
taking a ferry across the Hudson
and on to Trenton, NJ.

And more laughter when I tell
about my dive bombing
at Floyd Bennet Naval Air Station—
with a stick with a nail on one end
that collected litter near runways
and put it in burlap bags.

That's how it was for me in 1945.
Those are my war stories
and my bravery was never tested.

I still love my country
and would have given much more
had I been asked.

★ ★ ★ ★ ★ ★ ★ ★ ★ ★ ★ ★ ★ ★

In time, I was discharged honorably, and since then have gone about my life, always being grateful to the GI Bill which enabled me to go to college. I have always been aware that though a World War II vet, my service to my country so pales compared to so many others that I am occasionally embarrassed. I gave so little and received so much from my country. What a blessing it has been to me!

BRIEFLY I'M UNDONE

I'm laid back in my recliner
looking at white clouds
that change their shape
as they pass by.

And I see the little white dog
that I lost three years ago.

I can't forget
that little white dog
no matter how I try.

If there's anything nearby
to remind me of his presence
it triggers memories
that cling so to my heart
and are so easily revived.

A touch of sadness comes
and briefly, I'm undone.

I CONTEMPLATE MY YEARS

I've been allowed another day to be
and I, indeed, am grateful for the chance
to do a little more the things I see
need me. My years can stand to be enhanced.

I'll take the meager gifts that I now own
and ply them well before I leave this earth.
It is my hope and prayer that I'll atone
for investing so little of my worth.

The pursuit of happiness beguiles
sometimes—perhaps not you, but folks like I
who found his talents late. It took a while.
I had no dreams, thus options were denied.

Old, yes—but not wishing to be young
I contemplate my years—what I have done.

BUTTERFLIES AND THOUGHT

Long ago—
not too long after
my time began
I started chasing
butterflies.
I could reach them
but could not
grasp them.
The fun was
not in the acquiring—
it was in the pursuing.

And now
with considerably less energy
I chase thoughts
in the same manner.

I'll go to the grave
having grasped little
but having
a good time in the chase.

DRIVING NORTH

Driving north from Florida
where spring is subtle
I was quite taken
by the burgeoning trees
and the flowers
that bloom in April.

I had almost forgotten
as I reentered the beauty
that I had left behind some time ago
to claim a warmer space
for my declining years.

I did not miss this season
until reminded of its grandeur
as once again I was immersed.

I hope my memory will fail again
lest I mourn too much what I have lost
when I return to what is now
my home.

IMAGINATION

Our Creator
has given most of us
paint brushes for the mind:
gifts of our imaginations
that we use
to embellish our realities.

We employ them
to make life more fascinating
or to increase its darkness.

Our imaginations thrive
in our early days
when our childlike ways
tend to employ them.
But they often are discarded
as our years accumulate.

We're more prone
to revive them
when the things we fear
intrude upon our dailyness
and in our distress
we become quite deft
in amplifying possibilities.

Often our worlds
need to be made
better than they are
and if we're good at it
we can touch them up
with alterations
made by our imaginations.

These paint brushes
can arm us with optimism
and can harm us with pessimism.
We use them best when they bless.

MEMORIAL DAY

I can remember the Civil War Veterans
riding in open cars—
too old to walk in the parade—over 90.

Walking were some Vets
from the War to End All Wars—
later changed to
World War I.

The Boy Scouts and Girl Scouts were there
and some fire trucks and police cars.

I was drumming in the marching band.

We got to the cemetery.
There were some speeches
and then some guns fired—
a salute to those
who gave their lives for the USA.

Then we marched back
to where we began, where by then
a baseball game had started
right next to our school.

There were many bicycles
with their spokes decorated
with red, white and blue crepe paper—
and Good Humor ice cream was sold.

That's how I recall it
and it repeated itself, it seems—
year after year until one year
when it happened
I was in Boot Camp
becoming a sailor.

MEMORIES AND FILM

There are places
that he cannot go to
anymore.

His parameters have shrunk
and though he still has spunk
he's not the man he was.

And what he does
is not the same as when his years
were few.

So now he calls on memories and film
to draw him back to yesterday.

That is one way he deals with time.

And though he finds much pleasure
as he measures many of his days gone by
he sometimes sighs
and wonders not about what was
but what's to be—
what he cannot see.

MEMORY LANE

Down by the sea that I see no more—
the sea close to me in my days of yore
are waters still lapping a now distant shore.

I miss the sea sounds and I miss the sea sights.
Sometimes I still see them while dreaming at night.
Sometimes I have amazing fantasy flights.

I'm watching some whitecaps slide under my feet
as I stand on the shore and I'm counting their beats
and I'm finding in memories something so sweet.

I'm walking along where the waves meet the sand
and I'm picking up sea shells that are washed up on
land
and I'm gathering memories, so simple yet grand.

If one is unable to unearth his past
where some recollections fade while some of them
last
then one is deprived of great mental repasts.

It is good to go shopping down Memory Lane
though what really happened might not be the same
as what you recall. But you're not to blame.

MILKING

Some seventy years ago
I milked a cow
and to this day
I now recall
how utterly pleased I was
when finally
I got the hang of it
beneath a cow
who stood quite passively
within her stall.
And though that was the only time
I milked a cow
I've milked all kinds of things
since then.

In these latter years of mine
I milk the sky and earth
for poems—
I milk my memories—
I milk my thoughts.

After you get the hang of it
it's fairly easy.
Today I've milked a memory
and share with you
with hope it resonates.

I still can hear the splashing
as squirts of milk
spilled into the bucket
encouraged by the way
my fingers grasped and pulled.

MY THANKSGIVING NOTES TODAY

I woke up feeling thankful for my school—
Hand School—
grades 1 through 12—
one big square building
with twelve classrooms
and a music room
some offices
plus a basement where we ate lunch
with 3 cent milk
and often macaroni and cheese.
Then on top, sort of a tower
where a nurse held forth.
I walked to school.
Thirty-two of us
became the Class of '45.
I remember the names and faces
of many of my teachers
and many of my classmates—
but not all.
There were reunions for a time
but they ceased awhile back.
Most of us are no longer
though I still hang on.
Maybe the others are all gone—
nobody keeps track anymore.

My school days were not my best days
but they are becoming better as I look back.
I had some good teachers—
some good friends.
Mostly forgotten
I try to bring up everything I can this morning
thankful for all the was-ness that is no more.

NO FIREFLIES HERE

"Fireflies, who lighted your lamps for you?"
It was in a song I sang in grade school
way back when I was small and shy.
Recently, the words flickered in my mind
as something triggered a memory.

Catching fireflies in clear glass jars
was what we did in some summer evenings.

Later in less agile times
I still remembered the lines of that song
and remembered running in the dark
when the days were long.

Whenever I saw those fireflies
I went back in time.

Now, where I live I don't see them anymore.
I had forgotten that I had forgotten them.
Until now.

Now I remember.

And now
even though my darkness is deprived
I can recall old times and I can still sing
"Twinkle, twinkle little star."

ON A CHRISTMAS EVE

On a Christmas Eve
some eighty years ago
I quietly descended the stairs
and peeked into our living room
to see my father
setting up an electric train
in front of our Christmas tree.

No one saw me.

And to this day
my sojourn downward
while holding onto the bannister
has remained a secret.

After the revelation
of a sure-to-be morning gift
I returned to my bed
but did not sleep much
the rest of the night.

I remember the excitement of that morning
and making the train go round and round its tracks.

I have no idea what happened to that train.

As my years went by
I found replacements for excitement.

So much have I forgotten
but some memories are gems
and they gleam forever
when seen by those
who cherish them.

RECIPROCITY

Through the window
next to my recliner
I see a vast lawn—
green and still growing fast
even in the midst of autumn.

And every time I see the mowers
manicuring the space I so enjoy
I usually turn to memories
gathering all the lawns I ever cared for
in the years I sometimes long for
when I had the prowess now denied me.

I started mowing lawns when I was twelve.
I pushed, earning ten cents an hour
and soon I earned enough
to purchase my own haircuts
from Joe the Barber.

He took my two quarters
and helped me to an elevated seat
so he could easily reach my scalp—
then clipped away.

Back then I thought that cutting grass
and cutting hair was a kind of reciprocity.
I liked that word
and thought I had it right.
But I was told that we had similarity
and not reciprocity.
Only if I cut Joe's hair
would there be reciprocity—
and he didn't have any.

REENACTMENTS

When a person harvests memories—
if he is old and able to explore
his many decades, it is plain to see
there's so much—and most he must ignore.

He focuses on tidbits here and there
finding joy but also disappointment.
He may lasso thoughts that caused despair
or rediscover themes of wonderment.

Such reminiscing is akin to prayer
as one in silence enters history
that only he can claim—must claim and bear
its weight with its attendant mystery.

He may easily distort his past
but reenactments are the things that last.

THE TOOL WE'VE BEEN GIVEN

I sailed on a lake some time ago
in a boat that I had made
with two of my neighbors—
men now many miles away from me
as is that boat we made then.

My mind often covets those memories
spawned when this century was new
and all of us still had the energy
to do the things we wished to do
and weren't troubled by limitations
that now we reluctantly have embraced.

But rather than cry at the losses
we do best by recalling and smiling
for that is the tool we've been given
that offers us great consolation
when our accumulated years
deny us the blessings
once almost taken for granted.

THE LITTLE ISLAND

There is a little island
near the shore
which I explored
once upon a time
before I knew
the little that I know now.

I rowed there
and built fires there
and cooked a bit.

I slept there
and looked up at the stars
and listened to the waves.

I can't recall what I thought then
but I know
that I have changed considerably—
for better and for worse.

I was a boy
and turned into a man
and then an old one.

The island that I once embraced
bears not a trace
of my adventures there.
But I remember.

THE ROWING MACHINE

The rowing machine
has brought my feet
a little closer to me
when I go
to put on sneakers
and socks.

In addition
when I close my eyes
and pull
I find myself on the old lake
and memories swirl around me
like mosquitoes.

MY "TAKE" ON THINGS

A SATISFYING LIFE

There's been a lot of talk
about the rich, these days—
about the fact that wealth
should be more evenly distributed.

That sounds quite appealing
to those of us
who've never made enough
to be impressive.

The fact that too many in our land of plenty
are plenty poor is quite distressing.

Since I am neither rich nor poor
I'm not worthy of disdain nor pity.

But this I know:
that I've not had the inclination
nor the proper zeal
to gather lots of monetary wealth.

Had I a sharper brain, my strivings
might have gained far more for me.

But I admit, I've had enough
to live a satisfying life.

BAD DOG

How did it happen
that dogs get
such bad press
in a panoply of negatives?

"Going to the dogs"
"Dog Days"
"Dog tired"
"Doggerel"
"It shouldn't happen
to a dog!"
"Sick as a dog"

The dogs
that I have had
have been best friends.
Many of my human friends
would claim the same.

So I have wondered
how it happened.

CONNECTING THINGS

My new footwear with Velcro
makes life a tad easier for me
as Velcro does for so many of us
who recall the years
of tying laces—learning how to
before we knew how to read.
Shoe laces were first tied
about 3,500 years ago.

Buttons have been around for 5,000 years—
far longer than any connecting thing
that I know about.

Zippers came to be generally employed
between World Wars I and II.

Most days we are involved
in connecting things
and tightening things—
bringing stuff together.

We often fail to realize
or we just take for granted
that our dailyness is blessed
with wonderful inventions.

CREATING MOUNTAINS

Sometimes
I make mountains
where there are none
because the flat land
where I live
can be boring.

I need
at least a hill or two
and I create them
by squinting
plus
a dash of my imagination.

If I were
a serious searcher
I would find miracles
in the ordinary.

But I'm impatient.

The minutia
that surrounds me—
that sometimes astounds me
also makes me wish
for something more.

So I resort to **make believe**
and often find such satisfaction.

DAYS

There are those days
when you don't want to do
what the day demands.
Days when you do it anyway—
and days when you can't.

There are those days
when you're not quite sure
you can make it through
in spite of what you do—
but somehow you manage to.

Maybe there are less days now
than there used to be
when you wake up with a smile
and anticipate a day's unfolding.

Yes, maybe it's tougher now
but you vow to do your best
for it's in your interest to do so
no matter how the days go.

FICKLE TIME

Time seems to be so fickle—
going slow when we are waiting
and speeding up when we are joyful—
even standing still—
stopping like a broken clock
or hastening as
the pages of a calendar
are torn off
without our permission.

When we've grown old
in retrospect we are amazed—
the mass of years that we've collected
feels as if it couldn't be—
as if there must be some mistake.

That seems to be my fate just now,
I can't believe I'm what I am—
an old man
still trying to understand.

HEARING AIDS

Here in the quiet of this room
I know that sounds are coming soon
for I will place within my ear
devices that I once thought queer
but now I much depend on them
to hear what other voices send
to reach into my inner ear
where sounds are then made very clear.
If I should ever yearn for silence
I can surely bring its ambiance
just by turning off devices
that have helped my audio crisis.
So I am fortunate for sure
that sound or silence I can lure.

I'M SORT OF BLIND

I'm not apt to see dust
on a window sill—
on a table or a counter—
on a television screen.

She sees dust in so many places
I've unintentionally ignored
and she deplores its existence.
It's even on the floor!

My sight feels all right to me
but I'm not good at seeing dust.

And in addition
there is this related visual affliction:
items that I seek
in the refrigerator defy my sight
when I'm looking straight at them.

I'm OK when reading books
and I can see the screen
that records my fingertips.

I can look through dirty windows
and focus on what's out of doors
when it's suggested to me
by the one I love, that I might use
Windex while I'm scanning.

I'm sort of blind
but thankful for the eyes
I've tried to use
for more than eighty-seven years.

IF EVE

If Eve
after the Forbidden Fruit event
had been as cute as
my latest granddaughter
who is almost four
God might have been displeased
with her willfulness
but He couldn't have punished her.
He would have had to hug her tight
and say "I love you."

Of course
not all of us are that compelling
and sometimes we need yelling.

But to be kicked out of the Garden
seems to me a bit much.

JUGGLING

Most of us are jugglers.

We juggle thoughts.

We take on some
and let others go.

Sometimes they get heavy
and yet we can't discard them.

We set others aside easily.

We forget some
and they never return.

Others emerge again and again.

How many I can take on at one time
I really haven't been able to count.

Maybe you can count yours.

And add me to your thoughts—
at least for a little while.

LEARNING TO COUNT

My attitude toward gratitude has changed.
Never much for counting blessings
I am finally beginning to keep the score
of my assembled gifts.

It took so long for me to learn
to count what heaven bestows.
At last I know.

In my remaining years
with some smiles and likely tears
I'll pursue the counting
I have overlooked before.
It's taken long enough:
four score plus.
But finally
I have learned to count.

MAYBE IT IS

As you can see
this is not a "selfie."

And yet
maybe it is.

What I write
reveals a part of me
wrapped in my poetry.

Whatever will be will be
and whatever I write
that is grasped by your sight
will offer you insight into me.

MY HOLY TRINITY

The three wheels of my trike—
the wheels that carry me smoothly
over the landscape here
have become my holy trinity.

As I roll along the asphalt—
sometimes gliding—
sometimes powered by ancient legs
I feel myself to be
right in the hands of God.

I've meditated in various ways
over my many years—
have had various religious experiences.

But few of those transcend
the way it is with me quite constantly
while moving upon my tricycle
across the flat land here
in Central Florida.

Back in my seminary days
I read and wrestled with
the concept of the holy trinity—
at last gave up.

I didn't ever think
I'd get it through my head
and finally I stopped trying.

But now, at last I've found
all the trinity I need, and
it leads me to divinity!

MY POLITICAL STANCE

I don't presume to understand
the arguments the politicians make.
I'm easily persuaded toward the latest "take"
and then will switch my point of view—
will give another pitch my due.
I've tried to read and read
to grasp the things I think I need
to understand
but get more confused.

However, if I turn to ask the Muse
to offer me a rhyme or two
and then a little thought—
the overture is not for naught.

You may think I ought to have
my mind made up
about November.
You likely could dismember
any logic I'd employ to state my case
of the impending race.
And I would listen
but with a mind that time's been kind to—
except that it excels in waffling.

PRAYER MATTERS

Many prayers are garnished
with the theme of hope—
tantamount to a wish list.

Folks pretend "If it be God's will"
when they articulate their overtures
to whatever shape they think God is
but they have their own desires.

The truth is: they know what they want
and suppose His or Her view of matters
is much the same as theirs.

My view of this matter
just now suggested
may differ greatly from yours
and you may even be quite certain
that I am wrong.

THE GOD PARTICLE

Many physicists recently rejoiced
because what many of them refer to
as **THE GOD PARTICLE** has been found—
a rejoicing perhaps akin to what
the wise men discovered in Bethlehem.

How this discovery will trickle down
to the likes of you and me
remains to be seen.
We can be pleased that their passions
have been rewarded.
Generally, it is a good thing to be excited.

Far removed from their intellectual prowess
I cannot comprehend the details
of the contributions to their happiness.

But I do know that these physicists will grow old
and I hope their savoring of their knowledge
of **THE GOD PARTICLE**
will equip them well to handle the inevitable.

WHEN WRITING POETRY

When writing poetry
it is good if
you can take the ordinary
and make it extraordinary—
if you can see miracles
in unexpected places.

And if
you find that too difficult
you can **make stuff up.**

WHEN THE RAIN CAME

When the rain came
I was reading.
I was needing
some quiet time
not to make rhymes
but to still my mind.

When the rain came
I allowed its sounds
to resound in my head
which led to my feeling much
gratitude for my solitude.

When the rain came
I turned off the light
and closed my eyes
and I tried to think of
not anything at all.

When the rain came
I was not the same as I was
before it enhanced my life.

You may not notice
the change in me that occurred
when the rain came.

I am tempted
to refrain from telling you
but cannot help myself
from trying to explain
that I know I am not the same
because the rain came.

OBSERVATIONS

A HALLWAY INTO DREAMS

Shortly after lunch
I lay down
and buried my left eye
in a pillow.

With my right
I looked out a window
and saw white clouds—
soft white clouds—
fluffy white clouds.

Soon that eye closed
and shortly thereafter
all those clouds passing by
moved through the window
and began covering me
like a pristine comforter.

What a way
to begin a nap—
a hallway into dreams!

A SINNER AT BREAKFAST

The weather forecast was devoured
by some of the motel guests
sitting with me in the breakfast room.
Others hung around the waffle machine
with the same kind of intensity
guaranteeing a high calorie breakfast.
I sipped my coffee
and watched some sleepy heads
just up from their beds.
I could not hear anything
for there was too much noise.

I judged, even though I shouldn't have—
there were lots of stomachs nearby
far larger than mine
into which were poured breakfasts
far larger than mine.
I could not help myself
and closed my eyes
and prayed for the sinner who was I
judging my motel mates.
I asked if we might all have
safe traveling.
Then I rose from my table
and threw the plastic coffee cup
away and got on with the day.

HE WASN'T PRAYING

At first, I thought he was praying—
that man walking along the shore
just above the water line—
for his head was bent.

As he drew nearer
I began to assume
he might be gathering shells.

Then, as we passed each other
I saw that his hands were
cupped around his iPod
and it seemed to me
that his electronic connection
drew all of his attention.

He didn't acknowledge me
as I walked by
and as I marveled
that a man could be here
in this place of so much beauty
and fail
to apprehend its offerings.

CROWS

When you see one crow
upon a telephone wire
it's likely that it's meditating.
It wants to be alone
to ponder its existence—
the kind of space we humans need.

When you see crows gathering—
all lined up in a row
they're readying to listen
to a crow preacher crow.
They constitute his congregation.

Then they scatter to the winds
and do what crows do
and you see them now and then.

But mostly when you see crows
they're sitting in long rows—
rather, clinging in long rows.
And you may wonder how they do it—
how they hang onto that wire so easily.

Before the telephone
the crows used trees
for silences and for crowing.
Their lives changed
when man strung wires
across his land—
but not as much as ours.

EACH ONE HAS A STORY

He was slumped over in a wheel chair.
He might have been asleep.
I didn't know his name.
Maybe he didn't know it either.
And to me he was a stranger.

But he has a story, as does everyone.
Just because I do not know its chapters
does not mean that I should dismiss him.
He may have had some glorious times—
may have once been filled with laughter—
may have often felt on top of the world.
And his sorrows may have deepened him.
Who knows?
Because I don't know doesn't mean
that I should turn from him
and only view him with pity.

So I look at him
as one who has a story to tell—
as one who is more than he appears to be.
And though life's endings often obscure
what a life has been all about
I think it is good to see beyond these things
and at times to see each man
as one with a story known to someone
who might still be there for him.

That is what I hope.

INSPECTING

I've been doing some inspecting
of my expecting—
that is, I am probing into
some of my ancient days
wondering when
I began to think BIG—
to think about what I might do
with my life someday.

So much I don't recall about
the dreams of what I wanted to be.

Now I'm on the other side of life
checking out what I became—
thinking that I never could have predicted
those years I now look back upon.

I suspect I am not alone
in these meanderings.

Sometimes they have
disappointment in them—
sometimes a bit of proper pride.

ISNESS

"It is what it is"
and sometimes that's too bad—
though it could also be a blessing.

I never heard
"It is what it is"
'til I got old
and shared a lot with those
who had as many birthdays
as I took on
before and after this new century.

We have more reason to complain
than when young and vibrant.

"Isness" refines our coping skills—
many we never knew we had.

"Isness" is relentless
and our attitude toward it
is important to resolve.

I confess
that it sometimes gets me down—
but then I look around
and extol the goodness I have found.

I'm called to offer praise
for I often stand amazed
at the life I've had—
all the good
and all the bad.

It now has pretty much
unraveled—
this world that I have traveled!

LONG ISLAND SOUND

There were
several architects and engineers
gathered on the sand bar
building sand castles.
They made joyful sounds—
laughter and shouting.
They ranged in age
from three to six—
a mix of boys and girls—
all there with no fighting.

I was sitting nearby
taking in the scene from my recliner.
I was sitting there before the tide got low
and watched the sand bar being born
mostly with the strength of lunar power.
Little waves lapped and yielded
and then the time was ripe for builders
whose mothers stood upon the shore
and watched and wallowed in the ambiance
that offered offspring the happiness
that rarely comes in such abundance.

I was there when the tide came in
and the sun went down
and the sand bar disappeared
along with all the children.

Later, I was there when the full moon rose
and lit the surface of the Sound—
its waves increasing when the wind came up.
It blew the light into a mesmerizing dance
staged just for me and I, entranced, found
that I could hardly hold the joy
within my meager heart.

MAINTENANCE

The tires on my tricycle
require my diligence
to keep them filled with air—
forty-four pounds' worth
which slowly dissipates
and needs replacing fairly often.

If the tires get soft
the energy required
to move along the paths I take
is more than I can easily apply.

So I heed reminders that
I'd better find an air pump
before I grunt too much
to move along my way.

Sometimes I wish that
the maintenance of my body
would be as easy as my trike.

SIT AND WATCH

The eastern sky is just beginning to
ease the darkness from the sky—
the sky, for me, now over the waters
whose lapping against the sandy shore
was a lullaby last night as I went to sleep
and are now a call to another day.

I don't know where
the gulls are sleeping now
but I know they'll soon be here
to glide and dive when they arrive.

And then the tethered boats
will be unleashed providing pleasure
even to those who sit and watch.

And sit and watch
is mostly what I do these days—
and, yes, I think a bit
of how it used to be
when I came here by the sea
long years ago
and how my world has changed
though the waves that lap the shore
seem much the same.

PASSING SQUIRRELS

In the middle of the bridge
I met the white squirrel
that I had met before
but never there.
I stopped and stared—
so did the squirrel.

I was quite willing
to lose the standoff
and eventually I did.

The little white creature
fled from the big man's threat
and turned around and ran.

That opened up my way
so I continued as before
but wondered why
I scare squirrels
when ibis and black ducks
act as if I don't exist
whenever I pass by.

SCANT

I paid scant attention to the sky when I was young.
I don't know why.
I paid scant attention to the land and trees
when I was young.
That I don't quite understand.
I paid scant attention to a myriad books
when I was young—hardly gave them a look.

I was very good at scant—
was scant with everything.

Just how significant was my scant I do not know.
But now that it's too late for so many possibilities
I look more closely at the sky and trees
and try with all my might to read.

Yes, I have regrets and occasionally get upset
but that won't help me much.

So now, each day I try to be less scant
than I used to be
and though I know that scant is not a noun
but an adjective
my object is to create a new noun
that defines how once I was.

And I thought you might be interested—
unless you're into being scant.

STUFF

I regret that I forget—sometimes!
My mind neglects to tell me
what I have stored
and it ignores my need for recalling.
I find that appalling!

But what is less so
is that I find I like to rhyme
much of the time—
not your need but mine.

I have found
that words with similar sounds
intrigue me so.
I look around within my head
when I'm in bed.
Instead of dreaming
I find that I am only rhyming.

Or when I ride my trike
around the paths here
I like to play with words—
and that's absurd—
but that's my propensity
you see.
That's me.
I cannot flee from similarities.

THE BLUR

When the wind began to stir
the clear reflections on the pond
began to blur—
the trees, the clouds, the blueness of the sky
were shimmering.

There was then in front of me
a vast impressionist painting
and I was there with none to share
the canvas laid before me.

When the wind diminished
all those reflected things
returned to what they were
before the ripples came.

It must have been
a day akin to this
but long ago
that swirled into an artist's soul
and then he knew he had to paint
the way things ain't
but seem to be sometimes
when water and the wind
are able to impress a man
moved by reflections.

THE BOTTOM SHEET

Putting a bottom sheet
onto the mattress
of a king-size bed
is something that
I never learned to do
'til after I became eighty-eight.

Rather late
the process joined my fate.

Lots of folks
never have had
this opportunity
because their lives
never reached eighty-eight—
or if they did
somehow they avoided
this challenging enterprise.

I marvel that
so many years passed by
before I became aware
of such bed care—
not only aware
but participating in the process.

So many things
have happened around me
that I have failed to see.

THE PEBBLE

The pebble
may have been there
in my sneaker
before I started walking
on a chilly morning.

But it did not
make its presence known
until I was well along
the road I often take.

I thought it might work its way
to a place less invasive
but it insisted on being known
and even seemed to grow larger
as I tried ignoring it.

I began to hope
that I could make it home
before tending to its extrication
from my sock.

There were no nearby benches—
nor even any nearby grass.

I was at last forced to yield
and I knelt on the road's edge
to tend to this intruder.

I was so focused on the NOW
that Buddha would be proud of me.

THE THOUGHT

As I was walking down the road
a thought began to chase me.

It finally caught up
and quite easily engaged me.

My mind was forced to yield
and I lost track
of where I was.

But I keep on going
automatically
for quite some time—
until that thought was satisfied
and finally fled.

'Twas then that I
became aware again
of where I was
and realized how far I'd come—
past scenery that I often see
but didn't see that day.

THINKING SMALL

They are talking about global issues on TV:
the politics of the Middle East—
signs of Russian aggression—
the disparity between the rich and poor.
And I am listening—sort of.
I am thinking mostly about the bacon
I plan to fry in a little while—
how I will cook it
turning it over, then over again
with tongs we have had forever.
When it is "just right"
I'll lay it on paper towels—
pour off most of the grease
and then break some eggs
and drop them into the frying pan—
letting them spread out
on slightly reduced heat.
I will turn them over with a spatula
until the whites stop running
making sure the yolks
are not overdone.
The dishes we will use
will be warmed in the microwave
to maintain a desired temperature.
We will enjoy the simple meal
with little thought of pigs and chickens—
nor of the universal themes
set by the evening news.

THWARTED RECOLLECTIONS

Do you recall those times
when you can't recall
but almost do?

When you know there's a recollection there
but it remains just below the surface
and cannot name it?

Your conscious mind is thwarted
and you feel an unidentifiable presence
that frustrates your intelligence.

It's a fish you almost caught but didn't—
one so close to the surface and teasing you.

Maybe in time, through much effort
you will catch it and be glad.

Maybe you'll forget all about it
and later land it on your thinking shores
even without trying.

PRELUDE TO HIS NIGHT

A SONNET WHILE THINKING IN MY OUTSIDE RECLINER

I recline in my recliner often—
the one that fits my body to a tee.
I think that it would make a splendid coffin.
Lying in it I get so happily sleepy.

Oh that I could leave the world like that—
to see the sky then finally close my eyes—
my destiny complete! So laid back!
What a splendid way to say "good-bye."

Of course, the family might not find this pleasant—
to step out back and find that I am gone.
But maybe an OK way to leave one's presence—
no eulogies or doctor bills or songs.

'Tis quite absurd to think like this, I know.
And yet admit: what a way to go!

A STRIVING ANCIENT BEING

The isness of my was
is less today than yesterday
because my memory
has somewhat lost its grasp.

When I reach for wasness
I find barriers
that didn't used to be.

So I am more deprived
of where I've come from
than in my earlier years
when my wasness
was more easily accessible.

There is little I can do
but mourn the loss.

But I will pray
that this loss of wasness
will not too much hinder
my being the best that I can be:
a striving ancient being.

ANOTHER CHANCE TO BE

We who have harvested many years
are not quite ready to add our cheers
to the way the world is now—
the one, for a time, we served in various ways
and today sit back with little more than watching.

Our legacies scanned now through our memories
before the eulogies commence
are enough to make us wonder
whether or not we've done enough
to warrant another chance
should there be another chance to be.

AS DUSK BEGINS

In some waning afternoons
I'm apt to sit and watch a shadow
slowly creep across our lawn.

A nearby rooftop
slowly hides the falling sun
and offers entertainment
for the likes of me.

Eventually that shadow
brings a little coolness with it
and I'm apt to shudder with its coming.

Then dusk more readily asserts itself
and I become aware
that I must yield to night.

DAYS ENDING

Some days linger—
stay around
longer than their hours
as if reluctant to leave.

Others seem to hurry
and soon you wonder
why they seemed so swift
with their departures.

Maybe nature plays a part
but maybe we do, too.

We cast our moods
into the moulds of time
and hasten or delay the sunset.

BUT FOR NOW

I like to look at the sky
as I look high.

I like to look at the grass
when I walk past it fast.

I like to look at the trees
in front of me.

I strive to take all of it in
with glee.

I am pleased to see so much
and often find ecstasy.

I have found
when I look around
so much that astounds me.

Oh, I have seen the sea
and I guess
it's much as it used to be—
but it is rising so
that familiar shores
may be no more
by the time I'm ninety-four
and maybe sooner.

By the time I'm ninety-eight
the state that I live in
may be no more
and that may also be my fate.

But for now
I can relate these things to you
and I'd better not wait much longer
for I'll not get any stronger
tomorrow—to my sorrow.

HAIKU #2

So fast it happened.
I got old. Call me "Old Man."
That is what I am.

Time—it goes so fast.
I did not grasp its swiftness.
Past my understanding.

Nothing I can do.
Too late for any changes.
Sometimes I get scared.

JOINING THEIR RANKS

If I remember correctly
(and I probably don't)
"they" were referred to
by those of us who referred to them
as "old folks" or "the elderly."

They existed
and I had some contact with them
but didn't think a great deal about
when I would become one of them.

And I shouldn't have
for if I did
I've had little time
for anything else.

But now that scene has shifted
and I see that my age
and even a lesser age
is often noted in the obituary columns.

Yes, I have become "one of them"
and am painfully aware
that I have joined their ranks.

But that doesn't mean that
I'm an unhappy old man
for I am not—except once in a while.

NOT READY YET

Sometimes when I awaken
I think of those who won't—
of those who planned tomorrow
and tomorrow never came.
They won't have to worry
and they won't have to fret.
Someday I'll be one of those
but I'm not ready yet.

REREADING

Rereading
some of my poetry
of a dozen years ago
left me troubled
but with
some added pleasure, too.

I'd forgotten
so much of
what I once struggled
to produce.

The quality
of what I wrote back then
has hardly been improved
in spite of years of practice.

And yet
my need to write a poem
has not diminished.

Though my years assemble
almost beyond expectations
my urge to court the muse
has not diminished.

Give me another decade
and I'll not recall these words
and may never claim them.

SLIGHTLY BIOGRAPHICAL

He was old and he yearned to be young.
A few years he hoped to expunge.
He changed what he ate—
that helped change his fate
and a few of his friends, they were stunned.

Some of them thought he was finished—
but they watched as his waistline diminished.
He exercised plenty
and he got well past eighty
when most of his flab was extinguished.

He's not trying to live life forever.
He knows that he isn't that clever.
But he'll spend lots of time
just flirting with rhyme.
That's likely his final endeavor.

PRELUDES TO HIS NIGHTS

The sunset
that most days
offers us much beauty
is slowly creeping north
this time of year.

It's choosing a different site
to bring on night
each time it comes around
to offer him the gift of dusk—
the harbinger of the ending
of another day.

While many treasures are denied
a man of many years
he may be capable of finding others
that often seem to be finding him—
reaching out toward his eyes
in various forms of sunlight
that are preludes to his nights.

SEESAWS AND HEARSES ARE GOOD FOR MY VERSES

As I walked into the funeral parlor
I knew what I was there for.

But as I looked around
before entering
I saw a playground.

That started my strange mind
thinking that
seesaws and hearses
make very good verses—
the swings and other things
made my heart sing.

I wasn't ready to die
and I was unwilling to try
a way to bring on my demise—
however, I've thought about it.

But I was beginning to plan
for the day when it was at hand
which isn't yet
though occasionally I forget.

And I forgot about the playground
and turned to matters
about my being under ground.

That taken care of
I looked at the playground again
and knew that
I must play around in my mind
(which is sort of a playground)
something about verses and hearses
and children playing nearby
with nary a thought
of what they were near to.

STANDING IN LINE

Recently
three
e-mails
brought me
the news
that three
old friends
who were
aren't anymore.

And
the next day
two more were added—
or maybe they were
subtracted.

Sometimes I feel
like
I am standing in line
and waiting
to be
not being anymore.

THE CLOUDS SURPRISED ME

I'm out there in our back yard
looking at the sky which I often do
especially when the clouds invite me.

I begin thinking about something
I recently read in the SMITHSONIAN:
"Why did Jesus happen
and when and why did he happen?"

I don't believe I'd have been interested
a while ago, and I don't really know
why I am intrigued so now
as I'm close to closing out
my ninth decade.
I'll be going back to the clouds
and may forget the question.

But it took me by surprise
and seems to linger longer
than I thought it would.

TURNED OFF

The ceiling fan made no sound
as it turned around and around
And when I turned it off
it still continued
going 'round and 'round—
but more slowly—
and then again more slowly—
and then more slowly still—
and then it hardly spun at all—
and finally it stopped.

There are those days
when I feel dazed—
when I feel that
I've been
turned off
but still I'm going
'round and 'round
but more slowly—
more slowly.

WHEN THE SHADOWS LENGTHEN

When the shadows lengthen
and I use imagination
I can make most anything
upon the lawn I look upon.

The contingencies of aging
have not deprived me
of the power to create things
that are not, but seem to be.

The long strips of darkness
that play upon the grass
grow and grow—
eventually meeting me
who goes out to see
the pending glory
of a sun that's going down
beyond the live oak trees.

I find my breathing is enhanced
as I watch the arbor dance
with swaying branches
becoming arms that whirl around.

I see the shadows pirouette
before they fade away
to close another glorious day.

WHAT A WAY

The golden sun is slowly sliding—
setting behind the live oak trees
that shape the western edges of my sky.

Its light begins to break in pieces
coming through the leafy branches—
flickering as the gradual turning of the earth
titillates its glow.

The Spanish moss that hangs
below the lowest branches
becomes a glowing fringe
that undulates as breezes
move it back and forth.

Quite suddenly some shadows
consume my colorful display.

What a way to watch a day
turn into night!

WHEN THE MOMENT COMES

When the moment comes
she said in a desultory way—
and then went on to delineate
the services provided.

When the moment comes
was apparently how she was taught
to discuss the **MATTER** with her clients—
the matter being our deaths.

She said it many times.

She was young, or so she seemed.
We later found out: a mere fifty.
She handled the subject gracefully
and we signed the contract
and we were assured that our ashes
would go to the place intended.

WONDER

A HEALING

I've watched the healing of my thumb—
was wounded by a table saw
whose blade responded to my carelessness.

Every day, for weeks
I've seen the healing process
contend with this intrusion.
It began by building scabs at first
and then beneath them
tissue was restored.

The pain was difficult indeed
but soon diminished but remained
reminding me that work was going on
though I did not order it—
the work of restoration
did not require my will.

Your thumb
you likely take for granted
'til its usefulness is lost.
And then you marvel
that it's nearly indispensable.

BREAKFAST

The corn flakes
poured easily from the box.
Who designed the box?
What machine made it?
Where did the corn come from?
Who planted the seed?
Who watched it grow?
Who did the harvesting?
Where was it milled
and turned it into flakes
that now assembled in my bowl?

I peeled a banana
and cut it and dropped its pieces
upon the flakes
which resided in a bowl I love—
a bowl that has a painted bird
that becomes flake covered.
The banana came from far away—
harvested by a stranger
whom I'll never know
and shipped from there
to some place near
and then brought here—
and some cashier then checked me out.

So many folks to make my breakfast happen!
I pour the milk
and note the picture of a cow nearby
hanging on a wall.
Dairies also come into play
as I sit down to eat
and use a metal spoon
crafted by another stranger.

I could expand the list of those
whose expertise facilitates
this morning enterprise
of sitting down—
imbibing my early morning feast.

DREAM LIGHT

Dream light is a miracle
that's likely gone unnoticed
by a lot of folks—
or perhaps I'm wrong.
Perhaps it doesn't matter.

When you dream
it's often dark
but one sees people, places
and all sorts of other things.

They may be conspicuous
or they may be vague
yet when one wakes from dreams
it's often dark.

So what enabled you to see?
Dream light!

You may remember
scenes and details
though they often vanish quickly
and they often leave you wondering.
But all of them were lit by dream light.

How it works, I do not know
nor do I need to understand.

But I can marvel if I wish to
and I do.

I CANNOT AFFORD

I held the cereal bowl
rather close to my face
as I spooned in Cheerios
and watched the refugees
who were starving
thousands of miles away.

With each spoonful
I was wondering why
I was so privileged—
why it was not I
who had to flee.

Well, every day begins
in somewhat the same fashion:
my wondering "Why not I?"

But I cannot afford
to keep such wondering
wandering through my mind.

So I let it go
and it fades away
as I take on new portions
of my day.

I'M EIGHTY-SIX

I'm eighty- six.
There are plenty of eighty-six year olds around—
some in great shape—others poor.
Who was the first man to become that old?
How long ago was that?
What did he look like?
What did he wear, if anything?
What did he eat?
What did he do all the day long?
With whom did he live?

Crazy thoughts, perhaps
but if they are running around in my head
I've got to do something with them.
So I am telling you and encouraging you
to have similar thoughts.
Maybe such thoughts will drive other thoughts
from your mind
and maybe this will be a good thing.
If not, no matter—just a suggestion.

The most curious part of this investigation
is the WHERE and WHEN and WHAT DID HE LOOK
LIKE?
If you and I go back this way together
we'll likely come to see that we're related.
Wouldn't that be a find?

IF ALL THE WORLD

If all the world were just like me
I wonder how the world would be.
It wouldn't get its grammar right
but maybe there'd be fewer fights.

If all the world were just like I
I wonder as the years went by
if there'd be fewer terrible wars—
the wars that you and I deplore.

If all the world were just like you
what do you think mankind would do?
The world might be a better place
to grace this wondrous human race.

IN THE MIDDLE OF THE NIGHT

In the middle of the night
as I was pondering the distance
between my bed and bathroom
I thought about the new planet
recently discovered
being about 560 light years from earth.

Now that's a long way
and even my morning walk
doesn't come close to closing in
on Kepler-10c's so many miles away from earth.

Light years are difficult for me to fathom
and in the middle of the night
they have no business invading
my fuzzy consciousness.

But they did
along with the fact that Kepler-10c
has a mass 17 times bigger than our earth
and it is mostly rocks.

Likely there is no one on it
trying to figure out distances.

++

A light year is 5,878,000,000,000 miles.
That's five trillion, 878 billion miles ...

LUCK?

I used to wonder
about those folks
who escaped the jaws of death—
why so many of their thoughts
became theological:
God spared you.
He has more work for you to do.
God really saved your life
and there is a reason.

Now that I "escaped"
I understand the desire
to embrace the theme:
divine control.

But
understanding the desire
does not preclude the thought
of just plain luck—
though that appears so bland—
not as attractive as divine intervention.

MORE TO MARVEL AT

When I marvel at what my fingertips can do:
just a touch and many poems fly out of here
to places far and near—
it is a different kind of marveling
than when I stand in awe before a sunrise
or pause to watch a white squirrel
climb a live oak tree.
The first option is fairly new.
I never marveled when I used a typewriter—
corrected its mistakes with white-out
and pulled the paper out—
folded it, put it in an envelope
addressed that—and then put on a stamp.
And, what would it cost me
to send a hundred poems
several times a week, to a variety of friends?

So there is more to marvel at now
in this dangerous world of shootings
and violence and terrorism.

I can see so much of that—
(the beauty and the terribleness)
by using that same finger—
the one that allows me
to touch your world
with words that I assemble.

MY GASPING

When I read that there were likely
several billion galaxies I gasped.
I could not take it in
nor would I ever.
Even if I were much more clever
I could never take it in.
Yet I've no notion to deny
for who I am to question
whose minds far transcend mine.
Even microscopic things
that exist beyond the power of my eyes
instill some gasping within my mind.
I'm not much good at understanding
but I'm an expert when it comes to gasping.

MY LAST SUPPER

It wasn't a dream
for I was already awake.

But my head was still on my pillow
and, da Vinci's LAST SUPPER came to mind.

I could see the disciples sitting there
and Jesus was in the center of the scene
my mind was processing.

To my astonishment, each disciple
was looking downward—
each one studying his iPhone.

I could not help but smile
and could not help but wonder
what was it in me
that made my mind wander so?

What a strange but amusing way
to begin my day
after a good night's sleep.

Next
I'll be seeing Moses
getting the Ten Commandments
on his laptop.

MY "NOW"

Why do I spend so much time wondering what will be
when there is no way that I will be able to see
how the days unfold until the days unfold—
yet that is the way that I seem to be growing old?

I do spend some time enjoying memory's lane
exploring the days of sunshine—the days of rain.
Those journeys belong to me, and some are shared
as my loved ones recall together
how much we cared.

But then, I'm always called back
to consider the NOW
setting aside my past and my hopes somehow—
zeroing in on the tasks that I need to do.
It's each day that I meet—and I must see it through.

There may come a time when I'll cease such
        pondering.
Perhaps it has already come, and I'm just
        floundering.

MYSTERIES IN THE KITCHEN

When I am cooking chicken
I seldom ponder the question:
"Which came first
the chicken or the egg?"

Nor do I mull over that question
when working on
sunny-side-ups in the frying pan.

But I've had times
when I've tried to solve
these mysteries.

But right at the moment
I am wondering
as I'm preparing to make soufflé
when man (or woman) first
became fascinated with
the difference between
the white of an egg and its yolk—
and then strove
to do something about them
in his or her culinary endeavors.

When I finally became proficient
in separating yolks and whites
and whisking up the white
until it became froth
I marveled at the outcome.

I still do, in fact
and am off to the kitchen now.

There I may also consider the dilemma of
pro-life vs. pro-choice.

Eggs should do that to you sometimes
as you're breaking them.

NEEDLES

What do you think about
when you don't have anything
that demands your attention
and perhaps your expertise?

Lately, I been considering
NEEDLES.

How in the world
do they make them
and put that hole in one end
and sharpen the other?

And if that's not enough
how about those needles
that inject us with fluids
or withdraw the same?

That slender hole
that runs their length
baffles my imagination.

Last week, I worked on
TOOTHPICKS.

What's next
I have no way of knowing.

READING AT ASSISTED LIVING

When she had help
being wheeled in
to be right next to me
I, the reader of poetry
welcomed her
and soon I learned
that she was ninety-nine
and nearly blind.

When I had finished
sharing twenty poems or so
she reached over to me
and gave me a warm hug
and then a kiss on the cheek.

I thought: How dear! How sweet!

And then I felt the need
to hug the others near—
and was amazed
at the magnitude
of their reciprocity.

And I wondered why
I ever wondered
if reading there
was worth the while.

ORDINARY SOUNDS

I hear the dishwasher now—
the washer and dryer
a short time ago.

When I was small
I never heard such sounds.

I was used to toilets flushing
and perhaps my father was—
but his father wasn't.

I heard telephones ringing
but that was rather new.
My father was a telegrapher
and dotted and dashed.

I'm sitting here thinking
about our ordinary lives
and how what we hear
and take for granted
until recently, wasn't ordinary.

The flat TV screen
picking up reflections
from across the room
can swing into action
with but a small investment
of my time and energy.

I've had nothing to do
with these changes.

Other people have.

All I do
is take them in my stride.

But I do wonder a bit
what sounds my grandchildren
will take for ordinary sounds
which I haven't even heard yet.

REALLY?

The sun doesn't REALLY rise
nor does it REALLY set.
The moon doesn't REALLY change its shape
as the days of a month go by.

So how many other things
aren't as they seem
that we've been taught to believe?

Some maintain that global warming
isn't what it's claimed to be
and I can't prove them wrong.

But others much brighter than I
suggest that we had best prepare
for what's in store
and I tend to believe them more.

By the time man has overwhelming proof
I'll be aloof and watching
from my pedestal in heaven—
or, will I, REALLY?

RE-INVENTING THE USUAL

The clouds are not impressive
in the early morning light
though they have been that way often
as the earth lets go of night.

The trees seem less compelling
as I walk along today—
I wonder if I've lost my wonder
as I walk along the way.

It is true, the birds are singing
as they have sung before
but I seem to have a tendency
to listen but ignore.

But it's not the world that's changing
for it's about the same.
It's I who've done the changing.
There is nothing else to blame.

So I had better re-invent
the thing I've lost somehow.
Tomorrow I will take another path
my inner self I'll plough.

SHADOWS PASSING BY

Beyond the river
tall grasses waving in the wind
picked up the shadow of a bird
moving across the vista
I have seen so many times.

I did not see the bird
but tried to find it in the sky
and wondered what I'd see.

The shadow left no trace
upon the grass—
no way for one to know
there'd been a creature in the air
progressing by.

I've seen some lives like this:
leaving nothing when they're gone—
as if they'd never been.

And I am forced to wonder
if the marks I've made on earth
have been like shadows passing by.

THE SUN SET

I often wonder
when I see the sun go down
when was it that the first man observed
that it didn't?

Had I lived long ago
I don't believe
I ever would have noted such
not being smart enough
to discover things like that.

There are so many things
passed on to me
by those who came before
whose genius blesses me
with understanding.

And when I see the sun go down
sometimes I think of them
just as I count my blessings.

THE WIND CHOREOGRAPHS

The wind choreographs the clouds
most of the day long
and when the sun goes down
man is often astounded
at the display of beauty
found on the horizon.

Not always, to be sure,
but so often that
he cannot claim disappointment
when the stage he enters
opens to him at twilight.

The west has gifted me so much
and taught me to find delight
in the offerings of the sky.

And though dark clouds
can thwart the wind sometimes
and though the wind
with too much power
can thwart my view sometimes
hoped for designs in the west
usually lead me to hold my breath.

Frequently the shows are so fantastic
I feel speechless—
yet they force me to use the muse
to convey my gratitude
for some of the wonders
here on earth.

TO BE

TO BE is a mystery
I often think about.
Do you?
I cannot fathom
(although I try)
that it began
some thirteen billion years ago.
That's what they say—
the folks who know:
astronomers.
If they had told me
"thirteen million years ago"
it wouldn't matter much to me.
The fact that I am here today
and likely have tomorrow, too
is quite enough
to blow my mind away.
When I try to grasp
what is not graspable
I think I find my God
somewhere in the middle
of what my little mind
can't comprehend.
It's not only TIME but SPACE
evading me that makes me
marvel in my ignorance
and stand in awe of life
and my small portion
that I'm allowed to ponder.

TO CEASE FROM WONDERING

Sometimes
when I consider everlasting life
and wonder how that plays out
I find myself considering
a peanut butter sandwich.

I know how to make one
and how to eat it
and there is no wondering about that.

So I set out to make one
and I cease from wondering.

The same thing happens
when I ponder the matters
of life and death.

Jelly doughnuts sometimes
enter my mind.

Maybe I think too much
about phenomena
I'll never be able to figure out.

But if I didn't
I might get too fat.

WHERE DO THE LITTLE BIRDS GO?

Where do the little birds go
when the fierce winds blow?

I look out the window—
watch the dark clouds come
that deny the sun—
and I don't see them run
or fly into the sky.

They're just gone
from the land and the trees
as far as I can see.

When the rain comes down—
comes down so hard on the ground
turning mud puddles into lakes
how could they not stay awake
and do what it takes to survive?

As I look out there and stare
and search for hiding places
I see no traces of their beings.

My seeing is deprived more and more
until there's no seeing at all
for the storm is one of the worst.

Where do the little birds go
when the fierce winds blow?

I don't know!

WOODBRIDGE & GOOGLE

Why I hadn't been curious
long before
I do not know—
but one day, recently
I started walking
on two bridges made of wood—
a new pathway
for my morning ambulations.

Suddenly, I remembered:
one of my first words: WOODBRIDGE.
That's where my Grandma lived
and Grandma once
was much the center of my universe.

Then I began to wonder
why I never wondered
about that bridge in Woodbridge.
But now, wondering
I sought my friend, Google
and Google told me it was
named WOODBRIDGE
after a man who bore that name
who blessed a place
just on the edges of New Haven.

Not satisfied, I gained more facts
as Google took me back and back
until I was in England in the 7th century.
It was then that
people started calling people names
from places that they hailed from
and so one day (it's surmised)
one of them was called WOODBRIDGE
because he lived
near some wooden bridge—
its whereabouts unknown
to Google and to God.

Now, as I tread upon
those nearby bridges here
I possess more knowledge
than I had before.

WHAT WILL THEY TALK ABOUT?

It used to be
when
we gathered with friends
that we discussed
our jobs, our children
and the terrible
state of the world.

Now we discuss
grandkids, their kids
and our body aches
and the terrible
state of the world.

We have changed so.
So, too, has the world.

When the children
of the children we discussed
become our age
what will they talk about?

THE EUCHARIST

God Almighty
grasped
the brilliant moon wafer
with His fingers,
slid it across
the star-lit night
toward the west,
took it from the sky,
dipped it
into the sea
and fed me.

Previously published in *East*,
by Russ Peery, 2001.

INDEX

A

F

G

H

I

PHOTO CREDITS

Photos by Joanne Vary Schwandes unless otherwise noted. In order of appearance:

1. [FRONT COVER] Sunrise, Good Samaritan Village, Kissimmee FL, 11 December 2004.
2. [WALKERS OF THE DAWN SECTION p. 1] Reflection of the sun at sunrise, Merritt Island National Wildlife Refuge, Titusville FL, 3 December 2006.
3. [DAWN'S PUDDLES p. 6] Rain puddle, Veterans Park, Good Samaritan Village, Kissimmee FL, 4 October 2012.
4. [CELESTIAL DELIGHTS SECTION p. 19] Evening sky display, Good Samaritan Village, Kissimmee FL, 19 August 2004.
5. [A CASUALTY OF LUNAR LOVE p. 20] Full moon setting in the west, Good Samaritan Village, Kissimmee FL, 29 November 2012, 6:44 AM.
6. [A PACT WITH CLOUDS p. 22] Clouds above Orangewood Place, Good Samaritan Village, Kissimmee FL, 4 October 2012.
7. [THE MOON'S HIDING PLACES p. 35] Reedy Creek Swamp at the Osceola County District

Schools Environmental Center, Kissimmee FL, 13 February 2011.

8. [EMOTIONS SECTION p. 39] Rainbow as seen from Nock Island. Good Samaritan Village, Kissimmee FL, 20 May 2013.

9. [HEARING AIDS p. 135] Old Russ at home reading a poem to friend Betty Vary, 24 May 2012.

10. [I STRIVE FOR EMPATHY p. 52] Spider web with dew, Cape Vincent NY, 28 August 2013.

11. [THE ZOOEY ZOO p. 70] Lion, National Zoo, Washington DC, 20 April 2014. Photo by Paula Posas. Used with permission.

12. [WE MOURN A LITTLE LIZARD p. 72] Florida Anole on Bird of White Bird of Paradise (*Strelitzia nicolai*), Good Samaritan Village, Kissimmee FL, 14 April 2006.

13. [FOLKS I KNOW SECTION p. 73] Russ & Merle Peery with Joanne Schwandes, Paula Posas, and Hana, Good Samaritan Village, Kissimmee FL, 18 December 2012.

14. [A LEGACY p. 75] 5-month-old Hana with baby rattle made by Old Russ, 23 August 2012. Photo by Paula Posas. Used with permission.

15. [PINK p. 82] Old Russ with youngest granddaughter. Reedy Creek Swamp at the Osceola County District Schools Environmental Center, Kissimmee FL, 21

October 2012. Photo by Russ's 5-year-old grandson, Quenten Erikson. Used with permission.

16. [THE SLUG p. 88] Miss Alex showing a slug to 3-year-old student Ben, Audubon Naturalist Society's Nature Preschool, Woodend Sanctuary, Chevy Chase MD, 15 January 2015.

17. [HARVESTING A MEMORY SECTION p. 93] Classic pineapple design doily crocheted by Joanne's maternal grandmother, Altheada Hiscock DeLano, in the 1940s, 5 December 2012.

18. [BUTTERFLIES AND THOUGHT p. 102] Gulf Fritillary on Zinnia, Resident Garden area, Good Samaritan Village, Kissimmee FL, 6 May 2004.

19. [DRIVING NORTH p. 104] Star Magnolia, Brookside Gardens, Silver Spring MD, 12 April 2014.

20. [MEMORIAL DAY p. 108] Soldier's Monument, Mount Rest Cemetery, Bergen NY, 5 October 2006.

21. [NO FIREFLIES HERE p. 116] Detail from a pillowcase made for Merle Peery by Joanne Schwandes, 31 August 2014.

22. [RECIPROCITY p. 120] White Ibis on lawn under ibis-like clouds, Putter's Pond area, Good Samaritan Village, Kissimmee FL, August 23, 2012.

23. [THE LITTLE ISLAND p. 124] Campfire at the cottage, Cape Vincent NY, 3 October 2013.

24. [THE ROWING MACHINE p. 126] Old Russ on the rowing machine, Fitness Center, Good Samaritan Village, Kissimmee FL, 19 March 2016.

25. [MY "TAKE" ON THINGS SECTION p. 127] Leaves and boardwalk, Gatorland, Orlando FL, 22 March 2006.

26. [MY HOLY TRINITY p. 142] Old Russ's early morning tricycle ride on a paved path through the golf course, Good Samaritan Village, Kissimmee FL, 28 March 2013.

27. [WHEN THE RAIN CAME p. 148] Rain at Putter's Pond and Nock Island, Good Samaritan Village, Kissimmee FL, 14 November 2012.

28. [OBSERVATION SECTION p. 151] Ornamental butterfly grillwork and shadow on wooden bridge, University of Florida Butterfly Garden, Gainesville FL, 31 December 2012.

29. [CROWS p. 156] Crows on a wire along Westgate Drive, Good Samaritan Village, Kissimmee FL, 29 October 2012.

30. [PASSING SQUIRRELS p. 166] White squirrel, Good Samaritan Village, Kissimmee FL, 11 May 2006.

31. [THE BLUR p. 170] Clouds over Lake Sunset after 8 inches of rain, Good Samaritan Village, Kissimmee FL, 10 October 2011.
32. [PRELUDE TO HIS NIGHT Section p. 177] Dusk on the Patuxent River, Solomon's Island, MD, 7 November 2014.
33. [PRELUDES TO HIS NIGHTS p. 190] Sunset over Live Oaks and Putter's Pond, Good Samaritan Village, Kissimmee FL, 4 September 2012.
34. [WHAT A WAY p. 198] Live Oaks, St. Cloud FL, 28 February 2008.
35. [WONDER SECTION p. 201] Wasabi Coleus landscape foliage, Silver Spring MD, 15 August 2014.
36. [WHERE DO THE LITTLE BIRDS GO? p. 230] Mockingbird, Good Samaritan Village, Kissimmee FL, 8 June 2004.
37. [WOODBRIDGE & GOOGLE p. 232] Wooden bridge to Nock Island, Good Samaritan Village, Kissimmee FL Saturday, 22 December 22, 2012.
38. [THE EUCHARIST p. 235] Moon over Wolfe Island, Canada, looking NW across the St. Lawrence River from the US side near Cape Vincent NY, 19 September 2013.
39. [BACK INSERT p. 250] RUSS PEERY, 17 October 2012. Photo by Eduard Wiescholek. Used with permission.

Russ Peery, Age 85